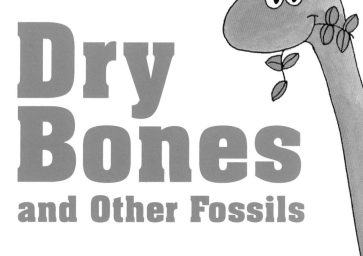

Dry Bones
and Other Fossils

Gary E. Parker, M.S., Ed.D.
Professor of Natural Science,
Clearwater Christian College

and

Mary M. Parker
Curator
Florida Creation Science Center

Illustrated by

Jonathan Chong *and* **Ron Hight**

Master
Books

Dry Bones
and Other Fossils

Revised edition
Fourth printing: April 1997

ISBN: 0-89051-203-5
Library of Congress Number: 79-51174

Printed in China

Contents

Dedication

To the Lord Jesus Christ, who blessed me with my wife, Mary, and our four children, Dana, Debbie, David, and Diane.

Introduction

Did you ever dream that you were hunting dinosaurs? Or that you found a lost valley full of all kinds of strange creatures, such as flying lizards and giant beavers?

Well, you can do it for real! Dinosaurs and giant sea scorpions and all kinds of creatures from the past are still out there just waiting to be found—as fossils! Fossils are parts of plants and animals preserved in rock. All you need to find them is a sharp eye, a small pick hammer, a sack, and a little background information.

To give you a little more background, I would like to use this book to take you fossil hunting with my family and me. I am Dr. Gary Parker, a scientist with training in fossil study (paleontology: pay lee on 'tol o gee). My wife's name is Mary, and our four children are Dana, Debbie, David, and Diane.

We have found more than a ton of fossils from all over North America and parts of Australia, Europe, and Asia. We would like to share our adventures and our thoughts about fossils with you.

So crank up your imagination, and we will take you on a fossil hunting trip with us! Ready? We have just stepped out of the car where the road cuts through a hill in southern Indiana. . .

Chapter 1

What Are Fossils? How Are They Formed?

Hey, Dad, what is this?

What does it look like, Dave?

It looks like a snail.

That's what it is.

Why is it so hard, just like a rock?

Actually, Dave, it's a fossil.

A fossil?

What is a fossil?

A fossil is a plant or animal preserved in rock. A very few were trapped in ice or tar, but most were trapped in lime, mud, or sand that turned into rock.

How did it get trapped, Dad?

Probably a flood did it. That's how most fossils were started.

What about this snail in my hand, Dad?

It was probably crawling around, just minding its own business. Then all of a sudden, "whoosh," mud from a river flood or from a big underwater landslide swept up the snail. So it was buried with all the other snails and clams you see around here.

Why didn't the snail just crawl out of the mud?

Good point, Dave. That's why it takes a **big** flood to start forming fossils. Mud or sand just settling out of a lake or ocean would never stop a snail, that's for sure.

What if the snail were already dead?

If the snail died and just fell to the bottom, the waves would break it apart, or it would rot or be eaten by other animals. The buffaloes shot by the cowboys and Indians never turned into fossils. The parts that were left just rotted away on top of the ground.

I get it, Dad. It takes something like a flood to start forming a fossil. The animal gets buried too deeply to crawl out, and the heavy layer of sand or mud keeps the waves or other animals from tearing it up.

Right, Dave.

But what made the fossil snail become hard like a rock?

You have watched people mix concrete, haven't you?

Sure.

What happens?

It starts off slushy when you mix the sand and cement and water. Then it dries out and turns hard.

Almost. Actually, the concrete cures, instead of drying out. The water helps the cement minerals stick together, and they lock up the sand particles to form a hard, man-made rock.

Okay, Dad. I know about concrete. But why is this fossil snail so hard?

First, the snail was trapped in the mud. Next the minerals in the mud started to stick together, as they do in concrete, and the mud turned into rock. Then, in this case, the snail shell dissolved away as the extra water was squeezed out. What is left is that rock in your hand, which is formed in the shape of a snail.

Is this a petrified snail?

Almost, but not quite. In a petrified fossil, the rock minerals fill in the exact place of some part of the plant or animal. In petrified wood, the minerals fill in all the spaces as the mud turns into rock. Look at all the details in this piece of petrified wood I have here in my pocket.

Wow! You can even see the rings!

You can see a lot on your snail, too. You can see the twists, and the hole where the animal came out. But none of the snail is really there. You have just a mold.

A mold?

What is a mold?

A mold is made when you push your finger into a lump of clay and see the outline. Here the mud was pushed up into your snail shell, and now you can see the outline of what the snail looked like on the inside. See this rock here?

Oh, yes. It's just a dent in the rock, but it still looks like a snail.

Right. This is an "outside mold" of the snail. When the mud hardened around the old snail shell, it took on the shape of the snail. Then the old shell dissolved away. If that hole had filled in with some other mineral, then we would have a "cast" showing the shape of the snail. Molds and casts and petrified things are all different kinds of fossils.

11

Here is another kind of fossil I like to keep in my pocket, Dave. What does that look like?

It looks to me like stuff that dogs drop in the yard, Dad.

You are almost right. Instead of dog dung, though, it's a fossil dinosaur dropping.

Ugh! Take it back!

Don't worry. It's a special fossil called a "coprolite" ('ko pro lite). It doesn't smell, and it can't come off on your hand. It has already turned into rock.

How about that! So a fossil starts when living things get trapped in mud or sand from a flood. Then when the rock hardens, the plants and animals that were trapped turn into fossils. Right?

That's right, Dave.

Here's another fossil, Dad. What kind is it?

That's a piece of coral.

Coral? I thought corals lived only in the ocean.

That's right. But all these other things lived in the ocean, too. That snail you had is an ocean snail. This is an ocean clam, and this is an ocean lampshell. Over there is a piece of squid shell from the ocean. This is part of an ocean animal in the starfish group.

13

How did all these ocean animals get to Indiana? Indiana is in the middle part of America, a very long way from the ocean!

Well, most fossils start out as plants and animals trapped in sediment ('sed i ment). Sediment is the mud or sand that settles from flood waters. Do you know of any flood big enough to wash ocean life hundreds of miles (kilometers) to Indiana?

Noah's Flood?

Sure, why not? The Bible tells us that the Flood covered the whole earth! Stories from tribes all over the world also tell about the Flood.

Did the Flood really cover the whole earth?

It surely looks like it. Flood sediment covers over three-fourths of all the land on earth. You can even find fossils of ocean life on top of high mountains. First, all the land was covered. Then, the Bible tells us, the mountains rose up, and the valleys sank down at the end of the Flood.

Did Noah's Flood make all the fossils?

The Bible doesn't tell us for sure. But the Flood would surely help us explain much of what we see. After all, fossils start as plants and animals which have been trapped in flood sediment. Then as the land rises and dries out after the Flood, all the mud and sand would begin turning into rock. And the plants and animals trapped in the sediment would turn into fossils.

Are any fossils forming today?

Any time a plant or animal gets buried under enough mud or sand, it could start becoming a fossil—if the mud or sand had the right minerals and conditions to turn into rock. But the rock layers with fossils we are standing on cover a big part of Indiana, Ohio, and Kentucky. There is no place in the world today where fossils are forming that way! This would take something like Noah's Flood for sure!

Why did God send the Flood that killed all those plants and animals?

That's one of the saddest stories in the Bible. It started with the sin of our first parents, Adam and Eve. Their selfishness and disobedience ruined the world God had created "all very good." Soon the earth was filled with violence. All this violence and wickedness grieved God's heart. The Bible even says He was sorry He made the world.

What did God do?

God sent the great Flood to destroy evil and give the world a fresh start with Noah and his family, as well as the animals they took on the Ark.

Are fossils the plants, animals, and people that were drowned in the Flood?

I think most fossils were formed during the year of Noah's Flood, and some in the big-area floods that followed. And you know what? If that's so, then you and I are standing right here on a huge graveyard. And all these fossils that cover the world tell us about the evil effect of violence and sin, and they remind us of God's judgment.

Will God ever destroy the world again?

Well, the earth is full of violence and sin again, isn't it? The Apostle Peter tells us this world will be destroyed by fire.

What will happen to everybody then?

That depends. The people who hate God will go on living in hate forever. But we can turn to God's Son, Jesus Christ, for forgiveness and new life. God has something very special for the people who are sorry for their sins and turn to Jesus.

What's that, Dad?

A new heaven and new earth, where God will live with His people, and where there will be no more sin and violence, no more pain and death. So, think of that the next time we go fossil hunting, Dave.

What do you mean?

All the fossils buried in the earth remind us how God hates sin and how powerful His judgment is.

But if God can keep His promise to punish sin, then God in Christ can save us from sin. And God will keep His promise of a wonderful new heavens and a new earth for people who love Him. Right?

Right, Dave. Fossils tell us about the same things we read in the Bible: a wonderful world created by God, ruined by man, destroyed by the Flood, and restored by Christ!

Chapter 2

What Kinds of Living Things Are Found as Fossils?

Was it easy to imagine yourself hunting fossils by the roadside with David and me? I hope so. I hope David's questions helped you to start thinking about fossils, too—what fossils are, how they are formed, and where fossils fit into Bible history.

But I imagine you still have many more questions. So did my youngest daughter, Diane. As soon as we got home, she started asking questions about the fossils we found. Before long, I had to take her down to the Creation Museum. We looked at the different kinds of fossil plants and animals there.

Do you want to come along? We'll stop by the house first and pick up Diane.

Say, Dad, is this the fossil snail that David found when you went fossil hunting?

It surely is.

David said this snail was drowned and buried in Noah's Flood. Is that right?

It seems to be. That's probably why we find fossils of sea life all over the earth. The Flood covered the whole earth.

You mean this snail was probably alive when Noah was alive? Wow! What other kinds of plants and animals lived on the earth back in those days?

Want to go down to the Creation Museum and see?

Sure!

(I hope there's a Creation Museum near you. Until then, get your imagination working again, and walk through the doors of the Creation Museum at the Institute for Creation Research in San Diego.)

19

Over here, Diane, is a display case that shows some of the ocean creatures we find as fossils. Do you see any you can recognize?

Yes, lots of them! There is a fish. There is a snail like we find at the beach.

Anything else?

Well, there is a razor clam, and a mussel, and, I think you call this one a scallop. That one looks like a starfish, and this one is a piece of coral. Dad, are you sure these are fossils? They look like the shells we found at the beach last Saturday.

They are fossils. But you are right, Diane. They do look like seashells today.

Why do fossil shells look so much like shells today, Dad?

Can you answer that? Just think a minute.

Hmm. Well, let's see. God created all the animals. So I guess if God created snails and clams, then fossil snails and clams should look a lot like snails and clams living today.

Good thinking, Diane! Now take a look over here. This mural shows the fossils of plants we find. What do you see?

> *There is an oak tree, a willow tree, and a palm. Over here is a magnolia and a pine, and there are lots of ferns. Do you mean fossil plants are just **ordinary** plants?*

Most of them are. Over here are some of the bony animals that were buried in the Flood. Like today, there are different kinds of fish and birds and turtles and bats and antelopes. So, from the fossils, it looks like snails have always been snails, oak trees always oak trees, and birds always birds.

> *So, the fossil plants and animals that lived before the Flood are pretty much like plants and animals today. Is that right?*

Yes. But some are different. What is that fossil on the shelf in front of you?

Ugh! I don't know. It looks like a pill bug, except it has great big eyes!

That's a trilobite.

A what-o-bite?

A trilobite ('try lo bite). It does look like a pill bug. It has a tough shell and lots of legs. But it also has big compound eyes like a grasshopper.

Neat! But why haven't I ever seen one? Where do they live, Dad?

They once lived in the ocean. But no more, Diane. They are extinct (ex'tinkt).

Extinct? Does that mean they smelled bad?

No. That means they died out. Judging from the fossils, the world once had many trilobites crawling around on the ocean floor. But no more. They all died off, or became extinct.

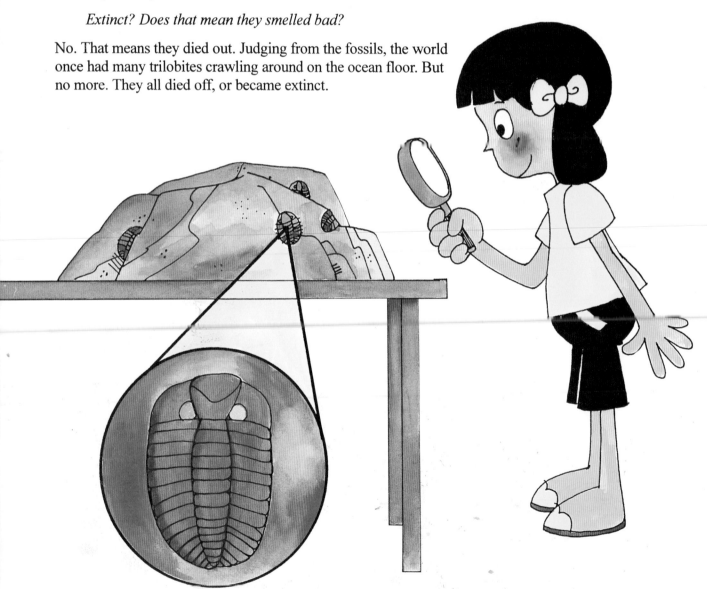

Why did they die and become extinct, Dad?

They probably died in the great Flood. Many water creatures probably survived the Flood easily. But trilobites lived on the bottom and couldn't swim very well, so maybe they were all buried. Many other animals probably also died in the Flood or shortly afterward. Remember when we went to the La Brea Tar Pits in Los Angeles, Diane?

Yes. We saw big, hairy elephants stuck in the tar, and a tiger with great big teeth!

There was an Indian woman, too. Those elephants and saber-toothed tigers lived in Los Angeles not too long ago, but they died out.

Why?

Maybe they couldn't live in the different climate after the Flood, or maybe people hunted them to extinction.

Here is a picture of another extinct creature, Diane. Do you know what it is?

Of course! It's a dinosaur! Did dinosaurs live when Noah lived, Dad?

That's what I think. After all, the Bible tells us that God created all the land animals the same day He created people. So God created dinosaurs, and, the way it looks, dinosaurs were drowned in the Flood, too. (There are now lots of great books for Christians that teach us more about dinosaurs.)

Wow! Man and dinosaur lived together! I guess that means they could have made footprints at the same time, too.

That's right. But if their footprints were made together, who do you suppose was chasing whom, Diane?

I bet the dinosaur was chasing the man!

Maybe not! After all, people used to hunt giant mammoth elephants with spears, and men with harpoons nearly hunted certain whales to extinction. Did you know the biggest whale is over twice as big by weight as the biggest dinosaur?

Really? I didn't know that. By the way, Dad, if dinosaurs were alive when the Flood came, did Noah have to take them on the Ark?

He surely did. God told Noah to take at least one pair of all the dry-land animals.

How did they all fit on the Ark?

No problem, believe it or not. Of course, Noah probably took young adults. But the Ark was so big, it could hold over 500 railroad boxcars full of animals with space left over!

Well, if the dinosaurs were on the Ark, why don't we see them today?

It could be the climate. Before the Flood, it was warm and mild and lush green over the whole earth. Did you know there are fossils of alligators and tropical plants in Greenland and Alaska?

Really? How did that happen, Dad?

Well, before the Flood it seems that there was extra water vapor in the air and more of that stuff called carbon dioxide. That would make the plants grow better and keep the earth warm, like a greenhouse.

So I guess the dinosaurs would have more to eat, and they could grow all year long. Maybe that's why they got so big.

Other things once grew really big, too: a dragonfly over two feet (60 cm) across, giant trees that look like the little horsetails and club mosses we have today, and a giant beaver over 6 feet (2 m) tall! While leading canoe trips down the Peace River near Arcadia, Florida, Mom and I have found parts of many large animals: huge shark teeth over 6 inches (15cm) along the edge, and the claw of a giant ground sloth bigger than a *T. rex* dinosaur!

Wow! Is that what the Bible means about "giants in the earth in those days?"

Maybe. There were also giant races of men on earth in those days. Only a few are that big today.

What happened to all those giant plants and animals?

A lot of them probably drowned in the Flood. Some of them were in the Ark with Noah. But, like the dinosaurs, maybe they couldn't find enough food or the right climate after the Flood.

Why did things change after the Flood, Dad?

It seems that much of the water-vapor blanket around the earth fell as rain during the Flood, so the earth isn't as warm today. And much of the carbon dioxide got tied up in the limestone rock that formed in the Flood. That affected plant growth and climate, too.

Are there more deserts and snow and ice today than when Noah was alive?

It surely seems that way, Diane. And before the Flood, there were many more plants without seeds, compared to seed plants. Plants without seeds didn't survive the Flood as well as seed plants. So maybe some animals died out because the plants they ate died out.

That makes me wish Adam and Eve had never sinned.

Why do you say that, Diane?

Then God wouldn't have had to send the Flood, and there would be many more plants and animals on earth. It might have taken three days to see all the animals in the whole zoo back when Noah was alive.

I think you're right, Diane.

28

Say, Dad, I was just thinking. . .

What?

Well, the fossils are good news and bad news.

What do you mean, Diane?

The good news is that fossils show how wonderful God is to create all the different kinds of life.

What's the bad news?

A lot of plants and animals became extinct because our sins made the world so bad that God had to send the Flood.

But there's still good news at the end, Diane.

What's that?

God told Isaiah that when Christ comes, "the wolf shall dwell with the lamb . . . and they shall not hurt or destroy in all my holy mountain, but the earth shall be full of the knowledge of the Lord, as the waters cover the sea."

I like that, Dad!

I do too, Diane! It is something we should always keep in our prayers.

Chapter 3

Why Are Fossils Found in Groups?

Did you enjoy the trip to the Museum with Diane and me? I hope you noticed that most fossils are ordinary kinds of life. They are just snails, clams, fish, fern leaves, and so on. That makes fossil collecting easier, since most things you find look like plants and animals living today.

But many of things have died out, or become extinct. That could be because of the Flood and the change in climate afterward. Many giant things became extinct, like six-foot (2 m) beavers, two-foot (60 cm) dragonflies, and those "terrible lizards," the dinosaurs.

And that reminds me. I promised to take you on a dinosaur hunt.

Here comes my oldest daughter, Dana, with a big bucket full of fossils. Maybe she found some dinosaur bones, and can tell us where to look. (I wasn't having much success, as you can see!)

Hi, Dana! What did you find?

I found a lot of clams, a bunch of different snails, some corals, a sackful of lampshells, and some trilobites. Oh yes, and some starfish parts.

Great! That sounds like a good find.

No, it isn't. I wanted to find a dinosaur bone, and I didn't find any!

You didn't expect to find any dinosaur bones here, did you, Dana?

Sure, why not?

Think a minute. Look at all those fossils you found: snails, clams, corals, and starfish. Those are all *sea* creatures.

Oh, I get it! Dinosaurs lived on the land. I guess you wouldn't find them with sea creatures, would you?

That's right, Dana.

Well, where can we go to find some dinosaur bones, Dad?

There is a great place along the northern boundary of Utah and Colorado, and a new area below San Diego in Mexico. And this summer we are going to hunt dinosaur bones in Alberta, Canada, near Drumheller.

Why do you find dinosaurs in all those places?

That's probably just where they got buried. As you know, plants and animals live in groups. Squirrels live in the forest; alligators live in swamps; and certain kinds of lizards live in the desert. So as the Flood waters began to rise over the earth, they buried fossils in certain groups according to where the animals or plants lived.

Hmm. So those places you named, Dad, are where the dinosaurs lived before the Flood. Is that right?

Almost. The dinosaurs probably got carried by the Flood waters quite a distance first. But at least those places would be near where they used to live.

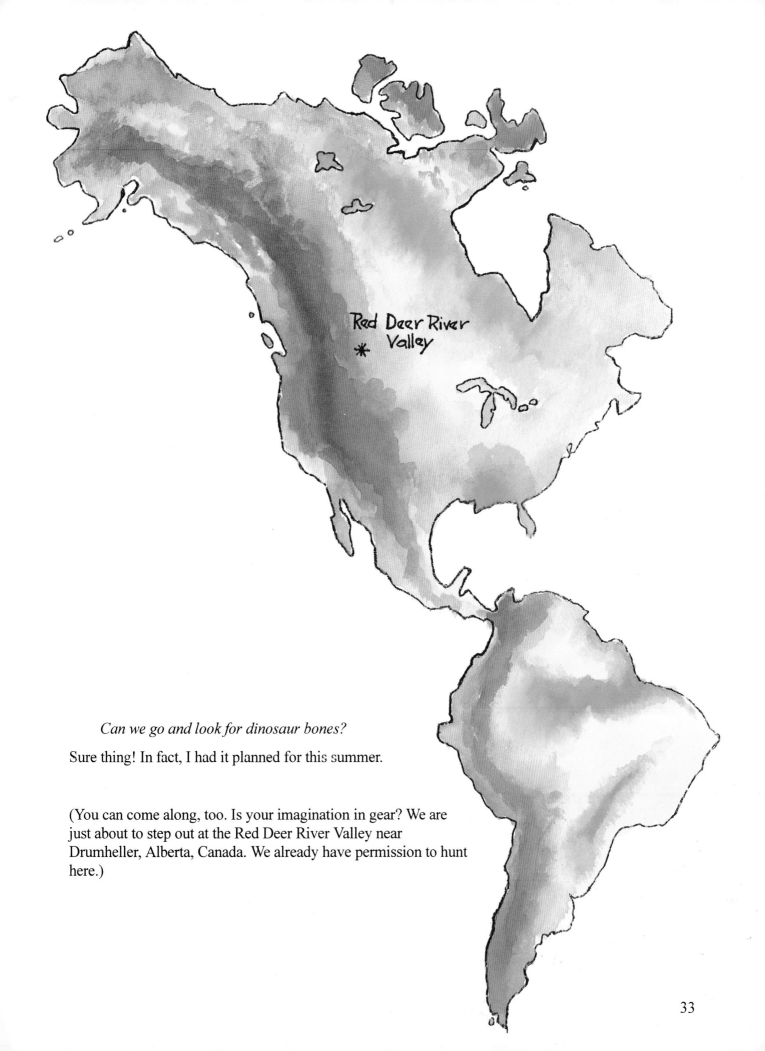

Red Deer River Valley ✳

Can we go and look for dinosaur bones?

Sure thing! In fact, I had it planned for this summer.

(You can come along, too. Is your imagination in gear? We are just about to step out at the Red Deer River Valley near Drumheller, Alberta, Canada. We already have permission to hunt here.)

33

Wow, Dad! Look at all these bones! I wish I could find a whole one! Can you tell what these pieces are?

Most of the pieces are really too small or too broken to tell for sure, Dana. But I think I can identify some. That looks like a piece of rib, and that big chunk is probably part of the backbone.

Come over here and help me dig out this dinosaur foot bone, Dana! Careful! We'll need to wrap it in plaster bandages, as Mom is doing with the big bone she found.

Great hunting, Dad! That broken dinosaur tooth Mom found was really neat—but I'm sure it will take her hours to glue it together.

We did get some nice specimens, but nothing good enough to report to the museum in Drumheller.

By the way, Dana, did you find any corals or starfish?

No, I didn't. I didn't find any lampshells or trilobites like we found in Indiana and Iowa, either.

Why not?

I suppose because dinosaurs and sea creatures didn't live together before the Flood. So, naturally, you wouldn't expect to find them buried in the same place.

I think you're right, Dana. So in a way, each group of fossils is an ecological zone (e ko 'loj i kul).

An ecological zone—what's that?

It's like a forest, a swamp, a desert, a lake, a prairie, or a beach. An ecological zone is just an area where certain plants and animals live. The fossils probably show us what plants and animals lived together in the various ecological zones in the world before the Flood.

So these bones we found here would be in the dinosaur zone, and the corals and snails and lampshells we found in Indiana and Iowa would be an ocean zone.

Right. Scientists even have special names for different fossil zones or groups. These dinosaur bones belong to the Cretaceous group. That's "Kree 'tay shus."

Are there other groups of fossils with big names like that, Dad?

Yes, Dana, about a dozen main groups in all. A group of fossils that is mostly trilobites and lampshells is called the Cambrian ('Kam bre un) for example, and the group with a lot of coal in it is called Pennsylvanian or Carboniferous (Car bo 'nif er us).

Dad, how was the coal formed?

Coal probably started out as a lush lowland forest, with lots of tree ferns and other fern-like plants.

Do we still have plants like that today?

Most of them died out, but we still have quite a few, mostly in wet or tropical areas.

What happened to the old coal-forest plants?

Well, Dana, as the Flood waters started to rise, the sediments first began to bury a lot of the ocean bottom creatures. Then as the Flood waters rose higher and the currents became stronger, they started to rip out the coal-forest trees and sweep them away.

Was it like a tropical storm, where groups of trees wash off in great big mats?

Yes, much like that. Some mats of vegetation have washed from the Amazon River 600 miles (1000 km) out to sea. In some mats after storms in the Pacific you can even see palm trees floating upright.

You mean the palm trees can be standing straight up and down? How do they do that, Dad? Wouldn't they lie flat?

Try this experiment, Dana. (You can try it, too.) Next time you are sipping a soda through a straw, put a piece of gum on the end of the straw and toss it into the glass. I think it will float upright. And that's the way with a lot of hollow-stemmed trees; they stand upright through several layers of coal.

So coal started as a group of trees ripped up and washed along in a mat by the Flood.

That's right, Dana. And there are many other things that make coal look like a Flood deposit, too. Some logs show the direction of current flow, for instance, and some ocean worms attached to the coal plants while they floated.

How did those mats of plants get turned into coal?

Well, the mats probably became buried under mud, sand, or lime deposits. Then the trapped and decaying plants gave off heat and charred. After all, wood is turned into charcoal today. And it takes only a short time, too.

Do you find very many animal fossils in coal, Dad?

Some, Dana, but not *very* many. Probably many of the animal remains settled to the bottom while the plants were still floating in the Flood waters. Besides, would you expect to find a lot of trilobites or dinosaur bones in coal?

Come to think of it, I guess not.

Why not?

Well, because the corals and coal plants and dinosaurs all lived in different ecological zones.

That's using your head! But suppose you found two fossil rock layers, one on top of the other. What would you expect on the bottom: the trilobites, or the coal, or the dinosaurs?

Probably, the trilobites.

Why do you say that, Dana?

Well, the trilobites are ocean bottom creatures, so they were probably buried first in the Flood. The plants and dinosaurs that lived on land would have been washed in on top of them later.

That makes sense to me, Dana. And you know what? Even if things started all mixed up, they might still sort out into layers.

How could they do that, Dad?

Let's try another experiment. (You can try it at home, too.) Put some water in a peanut butter jar (plastic is best for safety). Then add a big handful each of gravel, sand, and clay. Then shake it up very well and wait for it to settle. What do you see? (What do you see at home?)

Hey! We have three layers! The gravel settled first, then the sand, then the clay. Could fossils settle out that way, too?

Could be! So even if the Flood mixed up some of the ecological zones, we still might get fossils in layers because of the way things settled out in the Flood.

I guess so. But, Dad, wouldn't the Flood sometimes mix up fossils from different groups?

Yes, it would. And sometimes that's what we see—fossil graveyards full of mangled bones from all over the place. For instance, there is a cave in Maryland full of fossil bones. Some of the animals lived in the woods, some on the prairie, some where it's hot, and others where it's cold.

I see. the Flood waters washed them all into the cave area. That reminds me of the shell pits in Florida where Mom likes to take us fossil hunting. There are jillions of shells with hardly any sand between them—snails, clams, and corals of many kinds. And there are big shark teeth, elephant ribs, whale backbones, walrus tusks, and camel teeth mixed right in with them.

That's right, Dana—a real mix of land life and sea life all dumped into a giant common grave.

I guess the Flood helps us to explain a lot about fossils.

It surely does, Dana. After all, most fossils start forming when plants and animals get trapped in some kind of flood sediment, like mud or sand.

And the Flood helps us explain why certain kinds of plants and animals died out and became extinct, too.

Yes. And the Flood also helps us to understand why fossils come in certain groups, Dana. That's why we know where to hunt for different kinds of fossils.

Yes, Dad. Things that lived together got buried together. I was just thinking, Dad. The fossils help us to believe the Bible, too.

Why do you say that?

Well, what we read in God's Word agrees with what we see in God's world.

That's right, Dana! Of course, we believe the Bible because it is God's Word. But studying fossils gives us a chance to put that faith into practice.

Chapter 4

How Old Are Fossils?

The Flood described in the Bible helps scientists to explain how fossils were formed, and why they are found all over the world. The Flood also helps us to explain why fossils come in groups, and why so many things have died out or become extinct since Noah's time.

But Noah's Flood happened only a few thousand years ago. And that probably makes you think of another question, which my daughter Debbie asked me, too.

Daddy, I have a question. How old are fossils?

Well, Debbie, nobody knows for certain. But, if the fossils are the plants and animals drowned in Noah's Flood, then they would all be about five thousand years old. So that's fairly old, anyway.

Does it take very long for a fossil to form?

Not really. In fact, it has to start very quickly. A plant or animal must be suddenly buried under a heavy load of mud or sand in a flood.

If I buried a snail shell in the back yard, would it turn into a fossil?

Not right away, Debbie. A fossil starts when something gets buried. But then you must have the right conditions for it to soak up minerals and change into a fossil.

How long does that take, Daddy?

That depends on the amount of water and the kind of rock cement where the plant or animal is buried. It could take only a few years, or maybe 100 years, or possibly 1,000 years at the most.

So I guess there is plenty of time since the Flood to change all the plant and animal remains into fossils. Is that right, Daddy?

Yes, I think so. Do you remember that horse bone Mom found along the creek at Oak Grove back in Iowa?

Oh, yes. One end of it was very hard and rocky just like a fossil. But the other end was sort of soft and squishy like a rotten bone. I guess it didn't take very long for that bone to start becoming a fossil, did it?

Not much time at all! If conditions are not right, a buried plant or animal would never became a fossil. But if conditions are just right, they could turn into a fossil in just a few years.

That makes me think about the jellyfish fossils Mommy found in Australia.

I remember those, Debbie. To go fossil hunting in the hot Australian desert, your mom had to wear a "cork hat" to keep off the "sticky flies."

Remember the jellyfish we saw washed up on the beach in Florida? At first you could see the canals and other markings on the jellyfish. But before long, they just shrank into a blob that didn't look like much at all.

But many of the fossil jellyfish Mom found in Australia still had their shape and markings very well preserved.

I think that means they turned into fossils very quickly, before they had time to rot.

That sounds right to me, Debbie. Think about putting your hand into wet cement.

If the cement is not too wet and not too dry, you can leave your hand print. But you only have a short time to make the print, or the cement will be too hard. Right, Dad?

Precisely! And that helps us to understand those jellyfish fossils. It seems they were washed up onto a wet sand that acted like a natural cement. The scientist who first found them said the jellyfish fossil prints must have formed in less than 24 hours!

Wow, Dad! That's fast for sure!

And the scientist didn't mean just **one** jellyfish fossil in 24 hours. He meant **all** the jellyfish prints in a rock layer that runs over 300 miles (500 km) across the Australian desert!

*Now that sounds like more than just **a** flood. That sounds like **the** Flood in Noah's time that we read about in the Bible!*

I think you're right, Debbie.

Now you made me think of something else, Daddy. If all these fossil rocks were made in the Flood, then they would be only a few thousand years old, right?

Right, Debbie.

Well, is that enough time to make the Grand Canyon? Wouldn't it take a lot of time to make Grand Canyon?

Either a lot of time, or a lot of water.

What do you mean, Daddy?

I've led many of hiking trips through Grand Canyon. Why don't you and Mom and I put on our backpacks and look first hand at some of the evidence that shows it was a lot of water, not a lot of time, that stacked up those rock layers and cut the Canyon. (**If you've got a backpack, come along with us!**)

Sounds great, Dad! I'll get ready now!

Look at those big boulders buried in this rock layer. They were washed in from miles (kilometers) away.

It would surely take a lot of water to move those big boulders that far!

Now look at the straight line between this rock layer and the one above it. The bottom rock was supposed to have eroded for millions of years before the other layer settled on top.

But millions of years of erosion should have cut gullies and stream valleys in the lower rock. Maybe the Flood just changed direction and dumped new rock-making materials on top before the bottom rock had time to erode.

Sounds good to me, Debbie. See those tracks Mom is looking at? They were made by animals walking up sand dunes formed underwater.

We already know that fossil tracks have to form quickly.

Now look how these rock layers in the bottom of the Canyon were tilted up and sheared off.

I see, Daddy. But I noticed that some of those rock layers are very soft and crumbly, while others are very hard. Shouldn't the soft rock be more worn away?

They should be, Debbie, **if** the tilted rocks were eroded slowly. It looks, instead, as if the Flood came through here so strong and fast that it cut through the hard and soft rock almost equally.

A lot of water, not a lot of time, huh, Dad? But why are those rocks tilted up on edge? Did earthquakes happen during the Flood?

Yes indeed, Debbie. Remember, the Bible says that the Flood started when "all the fountains of the great deep burst forth." And at the end of the Flood, "the mountains rose up and the valleys sank down."

Wow! So Grand Canyon started as sort of an earthquake fault.

Perhaps. Grand Canyon is cut through a ridge that acted as a natural dam over 8,000 ft. (2500 m) high. Something, maybe an earthquake, cracked the dam, and the trapped Flood waters rushed into the crack, scooping out huge amounts of sediment.

And that would make most of the Canyon form very fast, wouldn't it, Daddy?

That's right Debbie. And, of course, further erosion has sharpened the features of the Canyon over the past several thousand years since the Flood.

I used to think it would take a long, LONG time to form fossils and things like the Grand Canyon.

Don't forget, Debbie, that 5,000 years or so since the Flood is quite a long time.

Yes. But many things that look like they would take a long time to form would happen much quicker in the Flood. Right, Daddy?

That's right, Debbie. In fact, Mount St. Helens showed everyone just how much even a *little* flood can do in a short time.

Mount St. Helens. Was that the volcano that went off in the state of Washington?

Indeed it is, Debbie. In one explosion the volcano produced a giant flow of mud. Then water flowing through the mud formed a small-scale version of Grand Canyon in just 5 days!

Say! I guess that proves for sure that it wouldn't take a lot of time for a lot of water to cut the Grand Canyon!

And that's not all, Deb. The walls of Mount St. Helens' "Little Grand Canyon" have mud, sand, and gravel stacked up in layers just like the rock layers in the "Big Grand Canyon."

And all those layers were stacked up in just 5 days! I guess the year of Noah's Flood would be plenty of time to stack up all those layers at the "Big Grand Canyon."

And there's more. The first explosion of Mount St. Helens produced a big landslide that rushed down into Spirit Lake and made a giant wave.

That sounds serious! A giant wave could do a lot of damage!

It did, Debbie. The wave sheared off thousands of trees and stripped off their leaves and branches. Some of the millions of logs now stand upright through layers of mud, making the logs look like polystratic (polly strat ick) fossils.

Polly-what fossils?

Polystratic fossils. Those are fossils that cut through many rock layers.

What is so important about those kinds of fossils, Daddy?

Well, sometimes a tree trunk or a big shellfish cuts across many layers of rock.

What does that mean?

Now, think a minute, Debbie. Suppose it took a long time to form one rock layer, then a long time for the next and the next. What would happen to the tree trunk or shell?

I guess the top would rot away or break off.

Exactly! But in these polystratic fossils, the top *isn't* rotten and the shell *isn't* broken!

Oh, now I understand. That means all the rock layers and fossils had to be buried in a hurry. Otherwise, the tree or shell would rot or break off.

That's right, Debbie. And there are many fossils like that in coal, too.

Daddy, that reminds me. Doesn't it take a long time to form coal and oil?

Not really, Debbie. They can be formed in a science laboratory in just a few hours. So a few thousand years since the Flood should be plenty of time.

What about those long, pointed things in caves, Daddy? Do you remember the ones we saw in Carlsbad Caverns in New Mexico and in those caves in Kentucky?

You mean stalactites (sta 'lack tites) and stalagmites (sta'lag mites), Debbie?

Yes, that's it. Don't they take a long time to form?

Not if conditions are right, and if you have a lot of mineral water. In one cave they grew so fast that they covered a dead bat before it had time to decay! Stalactites grow rapidly even under buildings and on light cords in caves.

54

I just thought of something, Daddy. Most fossils were trapped in Noah's Flood, right? That means they were alive when Noah was alive. So that means dinosaurs and trilobites and people all lived at the same time! Is that true?

It surely seems to be, Debbie. The Bible tells us about one man who lived with dinosaurs—Job. Job had seen a large land dinosaur called Behemoth, and he knew about a giant reptile dinosaur called Leviathan that lived in the sea.

Did any other people in history see live dinosaurs?

Yes. There was Alexander the Great, the famous Greek history writer named Herodotus, and a scientist named Aldrovandus, to name just a few. The scientist had even studied a small dinosaur that a farmer had killed. In 1977, Japanese fishermen netted the body of a large sea creature that had just died. It looked like a swimming "dinosaur" called a plesiosaur (please ee o saur).

Okay, Daddy. But I still have one more question. Why is it that so many people say fossils are millions of years old?

There are many different reasons, Debbie. For one thing, if you didn't believe in God, you would probably have to believe fossils are very old.

Why is that?

Well, if you didn't believe God created life, then you would have to believe that life made itself by chance. It takes a long time to make something by chance. Imagine how much longer it would take to *shake* together a jig-saw puzzle by chance than to put one together on purpose!

But if God created things like He says in the Bible, that wouldn't take so long, would it, Daddy?

No, it wouldn't, Debbie. The Bible tells us that God created all the different kinds of life in a short time. And He made them to live and multiply together in harmony.

And that's what fossils tell us, too! We just find different varieties of the plants and animals God created, like we have today. And they lived in ecological zones much like we have today, too!

Yes, except for extinction. Because of sin and selfishness, the world was ruined, and God destroyed that first sinful world with the Flood.

And that's what fossils tell us, too! Most fossils are plants and animals that were drowned and buried in the Flood.

That's right, Debbie. But that's not the end of the story. What does the Bible tell us about the future?

That Jesus Christ will come again and make all things new!

Amen, Debbie! "Even so, come quickly, Lord Jesus."

Chapter 5

Fossils —
Evolution or Creation?

My family and I surely enjoyed taking your imagination on some fossil hunting trips with us. (Maybe we'll even see you at the Creation Museum sometime, or out on the fossil hunting trail, maybe hiking in Grand Canyon, or canoeing in Florida!)

I also hope you have seen that the things we know about fossils agree with what we read in God's Word, the Bible.

But you have probably heard about another view, too. It's called "evolution" (ev o 'lu shun). My son, David, was asking me about that.

> *Dad, we have been talking a lot about fossils and Creation and the Flood.*

Sounds like you have a question, Dave.

Well, I was telling a friend at school about fossils. He said that we are all wrong. He said that fossils prove evolution.

A lot of people believe that.

What is evolution, anyway?

According to evolution, Dave, life started just by chance, and living things began to kill each other. Chance, struggle, and death are supposed to make things change for the better, so that some fish "evolve" into lizards, then into hairy animals, apes, and man.

That's quite a story! So evolution says death and accident made some animals gradually change into people?

That's the idea.

If that's the evolution idea, Dad, what is the creation idea?

The Bible tells us that God created a wonderful world with complex kinds of life all living in peace. Then man's sin and selfishness brought pain, death, and violence. The Flood destroyed that evil world and buried most of the plants and animals we now find as fossils. But God saved Noah and those on the Ark, just as Jesus can save us from sin and death today. And Jesus is coming again to make a new world of peace and joy.

That's quite a different idea! Do the fossils prove evolution or the Bible?

They don't **prove** either idea, but they really give far better support to the Bible.

*That's what **you** say, Dad. The people who believe in evolution probably think the fossils support their idea.*

Not all of them. Many famous evolution believers feel the fossils hurt evolution and help creation. Did you ever hear of Charles Darwin?

I think so. Isn't he the man that thought up the idea of evolution?

Yes, he is. Do you know what Darwin thought about fossils, David?

I guess he thought fossils were proof for evolution.

No. Just the opposite. Darwin said that fossils were "perhaps the most obvious and serious objection" to his theory.

Really, Dad? Why did he say that?

Because he knew the same things about fossils that we know, Dave.

What's that?

Well, you've found many fossil snails and clams and trilobites. Did you ever find a "snam" or a "clamobite," or something in between a snail and a clam, or between a clam and a trilobite?

No, Dad. Don't be silly!

I'm not, Dave. If evolution were true, then there should be fossils to show how one kind of life changed into another.

Oh, yes, I understand now. All we find are clams and snails and things, with no in-between forms. So I guess that would be evidence for creation. Right, Dad?

That's right, David.

What do people who believe in evolution say about in-between forms?

Well, David, evolutionists know that you don't find the in-between forms. They call them **"missing links."** Some evolutionists are still looking for missing links. But many scientists nowadays say that nobody will ever find missing links for evolution. After all, snails, clams, jellyfish, and complex squids are the "first" or "deepest" fossils we find.

What about plants? Did anyone ever find missing links for plants?

No. Darwin knew that, too. He called the origin of flowering plants a "mystery."

Now I remember! The seed plants we find as fossils are just oaks, willows, pines, palms, and plants like we have today.

That's right, David. Dr. Corner, a scientist at a famous university, once said, ". . . to the unprejudiced, the fossil record of plants is in favor of special creation."

*Don't people who believe in evolution have **any** evidence for their side, Dad?*

Maybe, Dave. There is one very odd fossil that appears somewhat halfway between a lizard and a bird.

It does? What is it called?

Archaeopteryx (Ark e 'op ter iks).

Archie . . . Archie . . . what?

Let's just call it the "Archie-bird," Dave.

That's okay with me, Dad! Does that Archie-bird really seem to be halfway between a lizard and a bird?

In a way it does. It has feathers and a beak like a bird. But is has teeth in its beak and a long, bony tail somewhat like a lizard.

I guess that does prove evolution after all, doesn't it?

Wait a minute, David! What about all the evidence for creation in clams and snails and plants and man and other kinds of fossils? It's not just one fossil, it's the whole weight of evidence that supports what the Bible says about Creation and the Flood!

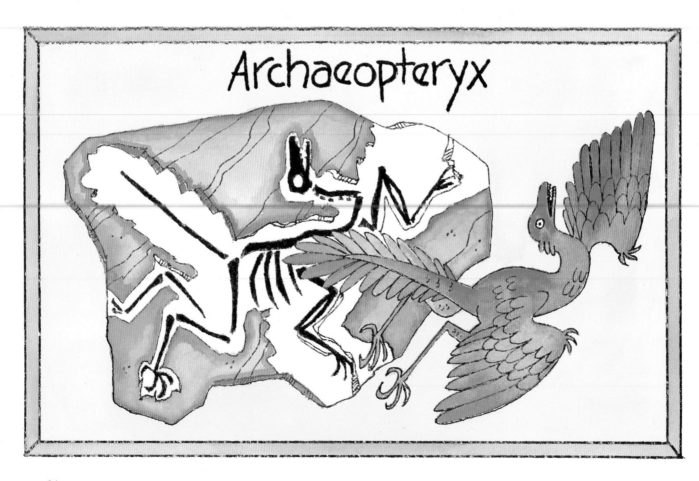

Archaeopteryx

Oh, yes. But what about that in-between lizard-bird?

First of all, it's not so in-between as you might think. Some extinct birds had teeth, and some lizards don't have teeth, so that's not so important.

I see. But what about the feathers?

Evolutionists believe that scales changed into feathers. But the "Archie-bird" feathers are all completely developed, just as those of birds living today. And their wings are completely wings, not half-way between legs and wings.

That's more like evidence for creation instead of evolution, isn't it, Dad?

It surely is. And there's one more thing, David.

What's that?

Recently, scientists found fossils of just ordinary birds **deeper** in the fossil rocks than the "Archie-bird."

Wow! I guess "Archie-birds" couldn't change into the first birds if birds were already here!

You're right about that, Dave. As far as what the fossils show, snails have always been snails, and birds have always been birds, right from the time God created the first of each kind.

That brings up another question, Dad. You were telling me that most fossils were probably things drowned in the Flood. Right?

Yes, Dave.

And so, those fossils were alive at Noah's time and are probably only a few thousand years old. Right?

Right.

Well, my friend who told me about evolution showed me a book. It said that fossils are millions of years old. He said you could prove it with uranium (u 'rain.e um) dating.

If you use uranium to date fossil rocks, Dave, *sometimes* you do get ages in millions of years. But did your friend also tell you about scientists at Oak Ridge National Laboratories?

No. What about them, Dad?

They used uranium dating on rocks of the dinosaur group and got ages of only thousands of years.

Really?

Yes, David. And besides that, scientists got dates of 169 million and 3 billion years for two Hawaiian lava flows. But these lava flows happened only about 200 years ago, in 1800 and 1801!

I guess uranium isn't proof after all, is it?

I don't think it is. And there's lots of scientific evidence for a young earth, too. But don't just take my word for it, David. You read what the Bible says, and study the science for yourself when you get older. I want you to know why you think as you do for your own good reasons.

You know, Dad, I was just thinking. If there isn't really any proof of evolution, why do people believe it?

Not because of the fossils, that's for sure! The fossils go along with Creation and the Flood. But I can tell you why *I* once believed in evolution.

***You* believed in *evolution*?**

Yes, I did, David. I even taught it in college (university) for several years.

Really?? Why did you believe in evolution, Dad?

I **pretended** there was evidence to make me believe it. I really believed it because I didn't believe in God. (You can read about Dr. Parker's change from evolution to creation, and from unbelief to faith in Christ, in his book, *Creation: Facts of Life*.)

You didn't believe in God, Dad?

Not really, Dave. I surely didn't believe that God was speaking to me through the Bible. And, after all, there is *one big weak spot* in the creation view.

What is that?

You can't believe in creation if you don't believe in a Creator. If there is no Creator, then creation doesn't make any sense.

But if there is a Creator, then evolution doesn't make any sense!

You are right about that for sure, David! Evolution is **not** based on the fossil evidence. It is really based on belief that you have to explain everything without God.

So creation and evolution are both really a matter of faith?

When you get to the bottom of it, that's true, Dave. If you don't believe in God, then you have to believe in some kind of evolution. And then you must try to make the fossils fit in with evolution somehow.

But if you believe the Bible, then you can see how easily the fossils fit with Creation, man's sin, and the Flood. Right, Dad?

Right, Dave! And that helps us believe what the Bible tells us about Jesus and how He can save us from sin and death and make a new world of peace and joy.

Just wait until I tell my friend that the fossils go along with the Bible instead of evolution!

Hold it! Wait a minute, Dave. Do you think that you can make your friend quit believing evolution and start believing the Bible just because the fossil evidence supports Creation and the Flood?

Sure! Why not?

Remember in John chapter 6 where Jesus was preaching right after He fed the 5,000 men? The people became angry and asked Him to do a miracle.

I remember. What does that mean, Dad?

It means that the people had just watched Jesus do all kinds of miracles. He even raised people from the dead. But just as Jesus said, "If they won't believe Moses and the prophets, they won't believe, even if someone rises from the dead."

*Oh, I see, Dad! You can't **prove** God to people. They have to have faith, and they have to have their heart right.*

That's right, Dave. But the facts of nature, like the facts about fossils, can help people come to faith.

What do you mean by that?

Remember what the shepherd David said in the Psalms? "The heavens declare the glory of God." And in Romans, the Apostle Paul said that God's power is "clearly seen in the things that are made."

So I can tell my friend all about fossils and the Bible, and maybe God will use it to help change his heart and open his eyes to all the evidence. Is that the idea?

It surely is, Dave. But go easy! Remember, your own Dad believed in evolution for years and years. Like Peter says, "Be able to give a reason for the hope that is within you, but in **meekness** and **gentleness**."

Okay, Dad, I'll try.

And we hope that you, too, will try to see God's world in the light of God's Word. The heavens declare His glory; the fossils show the power of His judgment. And the open arms of Jesus takes us in with the love of God that leads to abundant life forever for those who believe in Him.

Thanks for sharing our adventures and thoughts on fossils. From our family to you and yours—May God bless you!

Chapter 6

Fossil Collecting Tips

Where to Hunt Fossils:

Most fossils are found in layers of sedimentary rock (Flood deposits!), namely limestones (ls), sandstones (ss), and shales (sh). The best places to find rock layers (strata) exposed where you can get at them are cliffs, creeks, road cuts, and quarries (all starting with a "k" sound!)—and some gravel driveways!

Good sources for specific local directions include rock shops, fossil and/or rock and mineral (gem) clubs, museums, schools, colleges, and universities, and your state's Geological Survey. Many states actually publish detailed road maps to fossil-collecting sites, which may even include pictures to help with fossil identification. Some quarries arrange special fossil-collecting trips, and may even provide guides.

Unfortunately, many sources of information treat fossils in an evolutionary view. But the fossils are real (and don't come with dates!), and your finds may help you share how fossils really tell us about Creation, Sin and Death, Noah's Flood, and our new life in Jesus Christ!

Legal Concerns:

There is usually no special permit required to collect fossils of plants and of invertebrates ("seashells" and other animals without backbones). A permit is often required to collect bone fossils (especially on public land), and such a permit can often be obtained from the state museum. *No* fossils may be collected from state or national parks. Check your local law at a college or museum.

Always Get Permission from land owners to hunt fossils on private property.

How to Recognize a Fossil

To recognize a fossil, look for DESIGN! Until time, chance, and erosion erase the evidence of design, fossil leaves look like leaves, and fossil snail and clam shells look like snails and clams—a reflection of God's work of creation.

Because of the minerals they absorb, fossils are often heavy and stained in bland earth tones. Bones are often broken and hard to identify, but they usually have smooth, regular edges, a spongy, honeycomb interior, and resemble bones in your body.

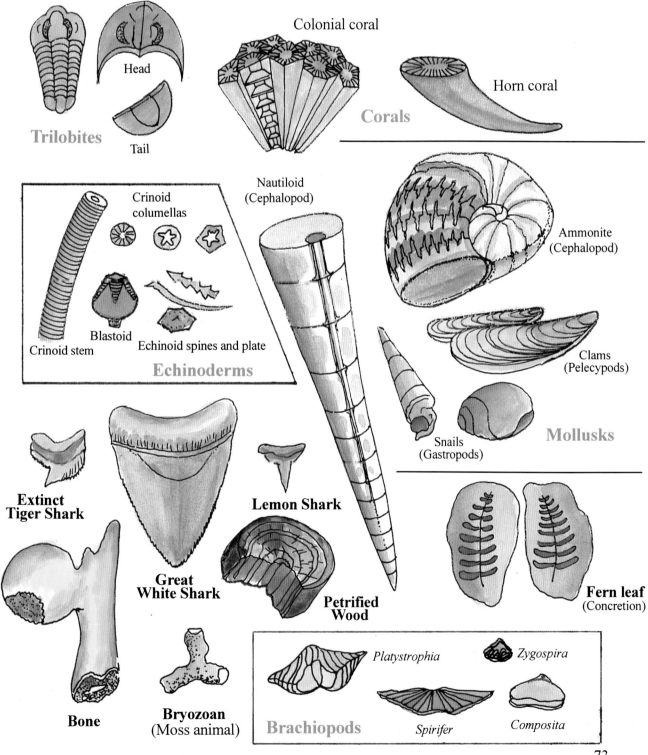

Trilobites
Head
Tail

Colonial coral
Horn coral
Corals

Echinoderms
Crinoid columellas
Crinoid stem
Blastoid
Echinoid spines and plate

Nautiloid (Cephalopod)

Ammonite (Cephalopod)

Clams (Pelecypods)

Snails (Gastropods)

Mollusks

Extinct Tiger Shark
Lemon Shark
Great White Shark
Petrified Wood

Fern leaf (Concretion)

Bone
Bryozoan (Moss animal)

Brachiopods
Platystrophia
Zygospira
Spirifer
Composita

73

What to Take for Collecting Fossils

The tools pictured below will get you ready for just about anything, but the tools you need will vary with location—and surface hunting requires few tools at all. Best wishes!

Don't forget: for your own protection, bring lots of water, food, a hat, and sunscreen.

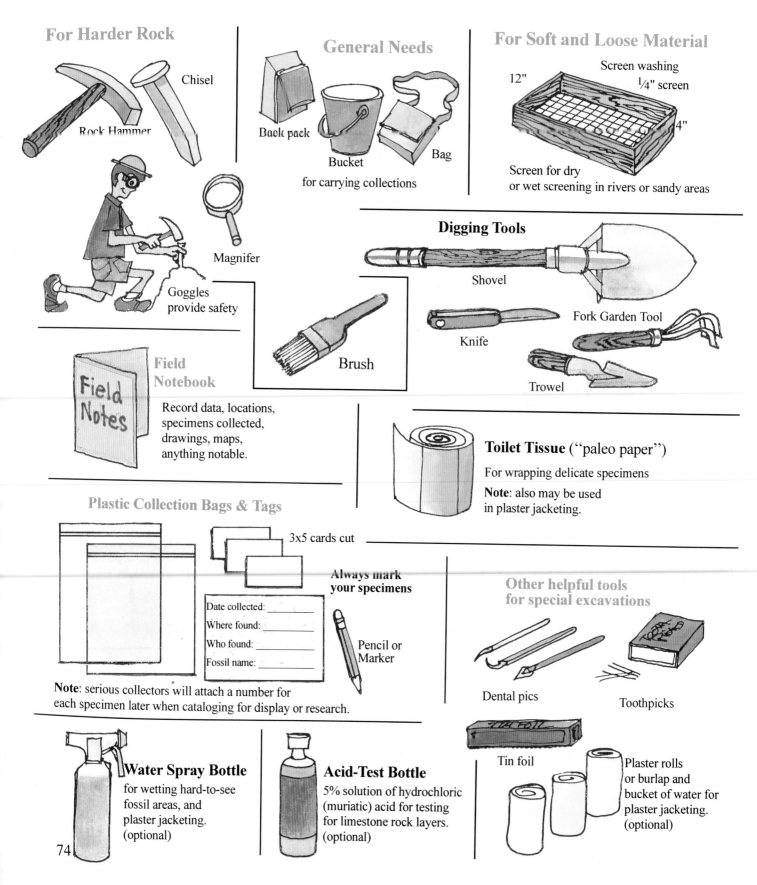

For Harder Rock

Chisel

Rock Hammer

Magnifer

Goggles provide safety

General Needs

Back pack

Bucket

Bag

for carrying collections

For Soft and Loose Material

Screen washing

12"

¼" screen

4"

Screen for dry or wet screening in rivers or sandy areas

Digging Tools

Shovel

Fork Garden Tool

Knife

Brush

Trowel

Field Notebook

Record data, locations, specimens collected, drawings, maps, anything notable.

Toilet Tissue ("paleo paper")

For wrapping delicate specimens

Note: also may be used in plaster jacketing.

Plastic Collection Bags & Tags

3x5 cards cut

Always mark your specimens

Date collected: _____
Where found: _____
Who found: _____
Fossil name: _____

Pencil or Marker

Note: serious collectors will attach a number for each specimen later when cataloging for display or research.

Other helpful tools for special excavations

Dental pics

Toothpicks

Tin foil

Plaster rolls or burlap and bucket of water for plaster jacketing. (optional)

Water Spray Bottle

for wetting hard-to-see fossil areas, and plaster jacketing. (optional)

Acid-Test Bottle

5% solution of hydrochloric (muriatic) acid for testing for limestone rock layers. (optional)

Plaster Jacketing

To collect large and/or fragile bones, try the technique here (perhaps first on a bone buried in your yard).

Materials:

Plaster of Paris	Rubber gloves	Foil
Water/Spray bottle	Bucket/Mixing bowl	Scissors
Hunting knife/Trowel	Paleo paper (toilet paper)	Permanent marker
4 inch x 4 foot Burlap strips/Heavy cotton		

Procedure:

1. Carefully expose specimen, digging around, removing the dirt, and leaving it on a pedestal 2"-4" high. On one side, allow enough space to roll jacket quickly over when completed. Roll-over area should be as wide as the jacketed material. (See picture on page 35.)

2. Cover the exposed bone with paleo paper approximately $\frac{1}{4}$-inch thick, making sure to cover the entire bone. Spray mist or sprinkle to moisten as you layer the paleo paper. This is to keep the plaster from sticking to the bone. Very important: every area of bone must be well covered!

   If there are any indentations in the bone after placing the paleo paper, take a little dirt and drop it into the indented area. This gives it extra support when the plaster is applied. (Foil may also be substituted here for tissue. Tightly wrap, making sure to tuck under bottom of specimen pedestal.) Then you're ready for next step.

3. Put on rubber gloves. Pour about 3 cups of plaster of paris into the bucket. Add water slowly while mixing, and bring to a heavy consistency, like thick cream.

4. Soak unrolled burlap strips in the plaster of paris. Working quickly, apply strips to paper-covered bone. Wrapping backwards and forwards over the top, make a tight fit, smoothing as you go.

   Apply as many strips as needed to make a $\frac{1}{4}$-inch plaster covering, more for a big and/or heavy specimen. As you complete it, wrap around the base part and tuck and smooth as you go. It should take 20–30 minutes to dry hard.

5. Write your name and the date on plaster, draw an orientation of the bone, record field location and field area with permanent black marker.

6. When plaster is dried hard, it is ready to roll. The material underneath must be loosened with a knife all the way around so that the bone is loose.

7. Securing and holding both sides so that nothing moves (even use 2 people), quickly roll upside down into rolling area. Do not attempt to lift or move—roll over only.

8. When dealing with very large bones, irregularly shaped bones or bones needing to be secured for travel, plaster the open side after it's rolled over.

Understanding Fossils

Fossils are dead things—billions of dead things—buried in rock layers laid down by water all over the earth. Fossils are ***fun*** to hunt and collect. They also help us to understand the beginning, history, and destiny of life on earth.

The study of fossils, like all studies in science, shows us that:

What we see in God's world agrees with what we read in God's Word!

Fossils tell us the same things about the history of life on earth that the Bible tells us.

The Bible describes the story of life in four stages, from beginning to end:

Creation: God created a beautiful world without struggle or death, and He created a wondrous array of living things to "multiply after their kinds" (Genesis 1, 2; John 1). That's why the kinds of life found as fossils always appear well designed, complete and complex, like varieties of the created kinds living today.

Corruption: Man's sin ruined God's perfect world, and brought disease, disaster, and death (Genesis 3; Romans 8). That's why fossils show death, disease, and a decline in the size and variety of many of the created kinds (the exact opposite of so-called "upward evolution").

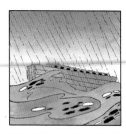

Catastrophe: The world became so filled with violence and corruption that God sent the Flood to destroy evil and give the world a fresh start with Noah and those with him in the Ark (Genesis 6-11; II Peter 3). That's why we find fossils of sea creatures on the tops of high mountains all over the earth.

Christ!: Fossils show us that God saved mankind from the awful destruction of the sinful world at Noah's time, so we can trust God, in Christ, to save us from the judgment to come on our sinful world. God created a perfect world, mankind ruined it, but Jesus Christ came to conquer sin and death—and He's coming again to make our world perfect and peaceful once again, to give us new and abundant life now and forever with Him. Fossils teach us we can trust what God tells us in the Bible about the past, so we can trust His wonderful promises about the future, too!

How to Display Your Fossils and Use Them Effectively

Cleaning and Preserving Your Fossils

Hard shells and bones can be cleaned with soap and water. Soak overnight (Tide works well), then use a *soft* toothbrush to remove debris. Lime deposits can be removed by soaking in 5% hydrochloric (muriatic) acid (***CAUTION!***—too much acid can dissolve the fossil). Use water to rinse off the acid, and keep baking soda handy to neutralize the acid in case of accident.

Bones often need special preservation. First, let the bone dry thoroughly. Then coat it with a preservative/sealer, or it will often begin to crumble. Elmer's glue makes a good sealer used as a mixture of 1 part glue to 4 parts water. Satin acrylic spray may also be used. The best sealer is Butvar, with an acetone base. Butvar can be used thick as a glue, or thinned with acetone to make a hard outside bone sealer. (Butvar may be obtained from a college or museum.)

Home Display

A fossil display can be a great point of contact and opportunity for Christian witness. You may be surprised how conversations may lead into historical and scientific evidences of Creation, man's sin, Noah's Flood, and the gospel of Jesus Christ!

There are several ways to display your fossils: a large or small glass case; framed wall display; mantle over the fireplace; wet or dry aquarium, etc.!

Parents, get your children involved in explaining the truths about fossils and Biblical history. Let young people be the ones to express ideas to visitors in your home. Training good creation scientists and creation museum tour guides for the future can begin right in your own home!

Praise God that there are a number of great books available for your study of fossils in Biblical perspective. The more informed you are (I Peter 3:15), the greater your opportunities and effectiveness in using your home fossil display. God bless you and your family in your fossil-hunting adventures!

Yours in Christ,

Gary and Mary Parker
Dana, Debbie, David, and Diane

Leading Children to Jesus Christ

During the late elementary years, boys and girls are especially open to a relationship with God. And at this time in their lives they are able to understand the significance of making a commitment to the Lord.

Here are a few steps you can share that the Holy Spirit can use to lead a child to Christ.

1. God loves you and wants you to become a member of His family. (I John 4:7–10)

2. Sin prevents you from being a member of God's Family. Everyone has sinned. (Romans 3:23)

3. There is punishment for sin. Because everyone sins, everyone will receive this punishment. (Romans 6:23)

4. Jesus loves you so much that He died on the Cross to take the punishment for your sins. (II Corinthians 5:21; I Peter 2:24)

5. If you want to receive the gift of Jesus' love, you must tell God about your sins and ask Him to forgive those sins. (I John 1:9)

6. If you ask Jesus into your heart and accept His love and trust in Him, His death means you won't have to be punished for you sins. Instead, you will become a member of God's Family and will have life forever. (John 3:16)

7. You should tell God and others about His great gift of love to you, in His Son Jesus Christ, and the happiness it brings. (Romans 10:9–10)

Remember: ***This is the most important choice a child or adult will ever make.***

Recommended Creation Science Reading

Children:

Bliss, Richard B., Gary E. Parker, and Duane T. Gish. *Fossils: Key to the Present*. El Cajon: Institute for Creation Research, 1990.

Fox, Norman. *Fossils: Hard Facts from the Earth*. El Cajon: Institute for Creation Research, 1981.

Gish, Duane T. *Dinosaurs by Design*. Colorado Springs: Master Books, 1992.

Ham, Ken and Mally Ham. *D is for Dinosaur*. Colorado Springs: Master Books, 1991.

Morris, John D. *Noah's Ark and the Ararat Adventure*. Colorado Springs: Master Books, 1994.

Morris, John D., and Ken Ham. *What Really Happened to the Dinosaurs?* Colorado Springs: Master Books, 1990.

Oard, Michael and Beverly Oard. *Life in the Great Ice Age*. Colorado Springs: Master Books, 1993.

Parker, Gary E. *Life Before Birth*. Colorado Springs: Master Books, 1992.

Petersen, Dennis R. *Unlocking the Mysteries of Creation*. South Lake Tahoe: Christian Equippers International, 1987.

Taylor, Paul S. *The Great Dinosaur Mystery and the Bible*. Elgin: David C. Cook, 1987.

High School and Adult:

Baker, Sylvia. *Bone of Contention*. Sunnybank, Queensland, Australia: Creation Science Foundation Ltd., 1990.

Gish, Duane T. *The Amazing Story of Creation*. El Cajon: Institute for Creation Research, 1990.

Ham, Ken. *The Answers Book*. Colorado Springs: Master Books, 1991.

Ham, Ken. *The Lie: Evolution*. Colorado Springs: Master Books, 1991.

Lubenow, Marvin L. *Bones of Contention*. Grand Rapids: Baker Book House, 1992.

Morris, Henry M. *Beginning of the World*. Colorado Springs: Master Books, 1991.

Morris, Henry M., and Gary E. Parker. *What is Creation Science?* Colorado Springs: Master Books, 1987.

Parker, Gary E. *Creation: Facts of life* Colorado Springs: Master Books, 1994.

Whitcomb, John C., and Henry M. Morris. *The Genesis Flood*. Phillipsburg: Presbyterian and Reformed Publishing Co., 1961.

If you would like a free *Creation Resource Catalog,* listing titles of other creation science books and videos, call or write: Master Books, P.O. Box 26060, Colorado Springs, Colorado, CO 80936, 1-800-999-3777.